CA for Christmas

A Treasury of 52 Favorites New & Old

Usable in Medleys or Individually

Created and Compiled by

Tom Fettke & Ken Bible

*Arranged for Choir, Ensemble,
or Congregation by*

Tom Fettke

Songbook Edition

Lillenas
PUBLISHING COMPANY
Kansas City, MO 64141

HOW TO USE
CAROLS FOR CHRISTMAS

Carols for Christmas is a compendium of standard, traditional carols blended with fresh, contemporary songs guided by two key words: *accessibility* and *familiarity*. Presented here is the full spectrum of the Christmas story, from ancient prophecy to contemporary application. All this within the reach of every choir and congregation.

Worship leaders will appreciate the thematic medleys and sequences appropriate for Sunday services and major seasonal events.

Choirs, ensembles, and soloists will cherish the variety of voicing options within each song.

Church orchestras will highly regard the creative, yet practical accompaniments that lend support and color to these arrangements.

Congregations will be thrilled with the opportunity to sing dynamic new texts coupled with familiar melodies.

The companion book, *Carols for Christmas Program Resources,* is a treasury of creative worship service, concert/ musical, and pageant ideas all based on the music of this compilation. No worship planner should be without this valuable aid.

Keep in mind that the arrows for performance found on the left side of many of the song verses are in accordance with the companion recording. If you use trax, please remember that these are the particular verses that are included there.

Here, then, is a collection of long-lasting, truly usable material celebrating the most significant birth in history. We love to retell the story, and we love to sing these songs. We're pleased to offer under one cover the entire Christmas experience for the total needs of your music ministry.

PEOPLE ARE SINGING, "JESUS IS BORN"

includes

Angels We Have Heard on High
Jesus Is Born
He Is Born

Presentation Suggestions:
ANGELS WE HAVE HEARD ON HIGH: Verses 1, unison; Refrain, parts; Verse 3, parts;
Refrain, parts; Choral tag
JESUS IS BORN: Refrain, unison; Both verses, parts; Refrain, unison, to Coda medley ending;
Refrain, parts, choral tag
HE IS BORN: Refrain, unison; Verse 1, parts; Refrain, parts, song ending; Verse 2, parts; Refrain,
parts, medley ending

Angels We Have Heard on High

Traditional French Carol

Traditional French Melody
Arranged by Tom Fettke

1. An - gels we have heard on high, Sweet - ly sing - ing o'er the plains,
2. Shep - herds, why this ju - bi - lee? Why your joy - ous strains pro - long?
3. Come to Beth - le - hem, and see Him whose birth the an - gels sing;
4. See with - in a man - ger laid Je - sus, Lord of heav'n and earth!

And the moun - tains in re - ply, Ech - o back their joy - ous strains.
Say what may the tid - ings be Which in - spire your heav'n - ly song?
Come, a - dore on bend - ed knee Christ the Lord, the new - born King.
Mar - y, Jo - seph, lend your aid, With us sing our Sav - ior's birth.

Jesus Is Born

Words and Music by
STEVE GREEN, PHIL NAISH,
COLIN GREEN, and COLLEEN GREEN

The bells are ring-ing, peo-ple are sing-ing, An-gels say with joy, "Je-sus is born!" There in a man-ger, He was no strang-er, Proph-e-sied, now ar-rived, "Je-sus is born!" 1. Be- (2. Be)-

He Is Born

NAN ALLEN
and Traditional

Traditional French Carol
Arranged by Tom Fettke

SING WE ALL NOEL

includes

Deck the Halls
Sing We Now of Christmas
Come, Ye Lofty

Presentation Suggestions:
DECK THE HALLS: Verse 1, unison; Ms. 13, parts, song ending; Verse 2, parts, choral tag
SING WE NOW OF CHRISTMAS: Verse 1, ladies unison; Ms. 38, choir unison, song ending; Verse 2, men unison; Ms. 38, choir unison, song ending; Verse 3, choir unison, choral tag, parts
COME, YE LOFTY: Verse 1, parts, medley ending; Verse 3, unison (opt. 2-part); Ms.67, parts, endings 1 and 2

Deck the Halls

KEN BIBLE and
Traditional

Welsh Melody
Arranged by Tom Fettke

14

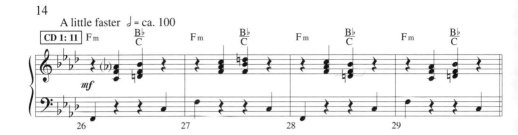

Sing We Now of Christmas

KEN BIBLE and
Traditional

Traditional French Carol
Arranged by Tom Fettke

> 1. Sing we now of Christ - mas, No - el__ sing we here!
> 2. Proph - ets sang of Christ - mas Long be - fore the dawn.
> 3. An - gels sang His glo - ry At the__ hum - ble birth.

Lis - ten to our prais - es
Now the Light is shin - ing,
Hear the song cres - cen - do,

To the__ Babe so dear.
And we__ join their song.
As it__ fills the earth.

Refrain

Sing we No - el, The

CD 1: 12 1st time
CD 1: 13 2nd time

King is born, No - el! Sing we now of Christ - mas,

Song ending
Choral tag and medley ending
Sing we all No - el! el! Sing we all, No -

Listesso ♩ = ♩ ♩ = ca. 100
CD 1: 14
el!

Come, Ye Lofty

NAN ALLEN and
Traditional

Old Breton Melody
Arranged by Tom Fettke

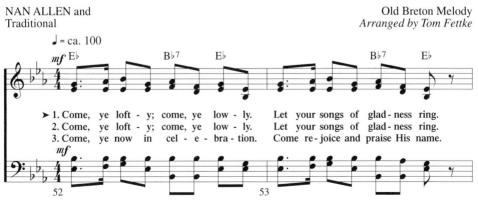

♩ = ca. 100

1. Come, ye loft - y; come, ye low - ly. Let your songs of glad - ness ring.
2. Come, ye loft - y; come, ye low - ly. Let your songs of glad - ness ring.
3. Come, ye now in cel - e - bra - tion. Come re - joice and praise His name.

EMMANUEL– GOD IS WITH US

includes
Jesus, Name Above All Names
Emmanuel
God Is with Us! Alleluia!

Presentation Suggestions:
JESUS, NAME ABOVE ALL NAMES: Unison, two times, Medley ending 2nd time
EMMANUEL: Men unison; Ms. 26, beat 3, ladies unison, Medley ending
GOD IS WITH US: Verse 1, choir unison, song ending; Verse 2, ladies unison; Ms. 42,
beat 3, men unison; Ms. 44, beat 4, ladies unison; Ms. 46, beat 3, men unison; Ms. 48,
beat 3, choir unison, medley ending; Verse 3, choir unison; Ms. 59, beat 3, parts; Ms.
61, beat 3, unison; Ms. 67, beat 3, parts

Jesus, Name Above All Names

Words and Music by
NAIDA HEARN

Medley Sequence copyright © 1998 by Pilot Point Music (ASCAP). All rights reserved.
Administered by The Copyright Company, 40 Music Square East, Nashville, TN 37203.

19

Emmanuel

Words and Music by
BOB MCGEE

His name is called Em-man-u-

el.

Song ending
Medley ending   rit.   cresc.

CD 1: 18   Listesso ♩ = ♩   ♩ = ca. 80

mf

God Is with Us! Alleluia!

KEN BIBLE, TOM FETTKE
and THOMAS KEN

Geistliche Kirchengesange,
Cologne, 1623
Arranged by Tom Fettke

♩ = ca. 80

mf ➤ 1. His   name   is   called   Em-man-u-el—   More
f ➤ 2. Re- joice   and   lay   a-side   your   fear.   Re-
    3. Praise   God,   from whom   all   bless-ings   flow.   Praise

HOLY CHILD...HOLY NIGHT

includes
Love Has Come!
O Holy Night
Holy Savior

Presentation Suggestions:
LOVE HAVE COME!: Verse 1, parts, song ending; Verse 2, unison, medley ending
O HOLY NIGHT: Verse 1, parts; Verse 3, unison; Ms. 56, parts, choral tag
HOLY SAVIOR: Parts both times

Love Has Come!

Tune: *Bring a Torch, Jeanette, Isabella*

KEN BIBLE

French carol melody
Attr. to Saboly, 17th c.

26

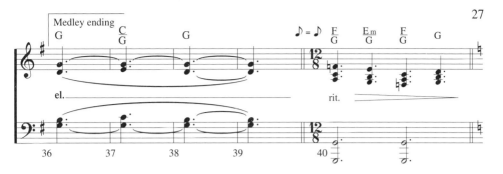

O Holy Night

JOHN S. DWIGHT

ADOLPHE C. ADAM
Arranged by Tom Fettke

28

30

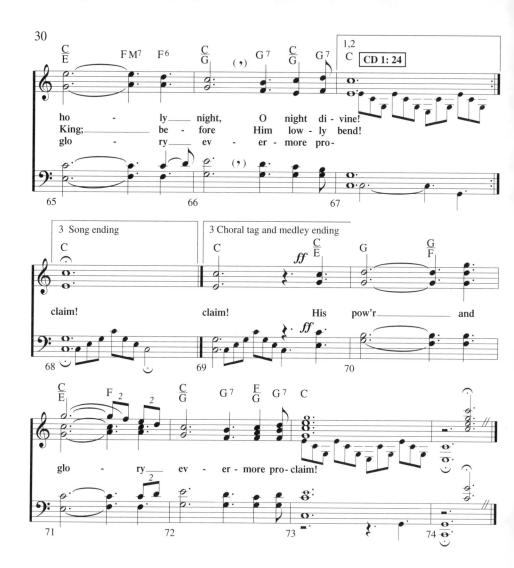

ho - ly___ night, O night di - vine!
King;___ be - fore Him low - ly bend!
glo - ry___ ev - er - more pro-

3 Song ending

claim!

3 Choral tag and medley ending

claim! His pow'r___ and

glo - ry___ ev - er - more pro - claim!

Holy Savior

Words and Music by
MOSIE LISTER

Worshipful ♪ = ca. 104

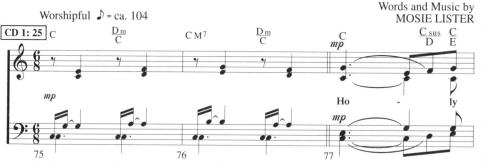

Ho - ly

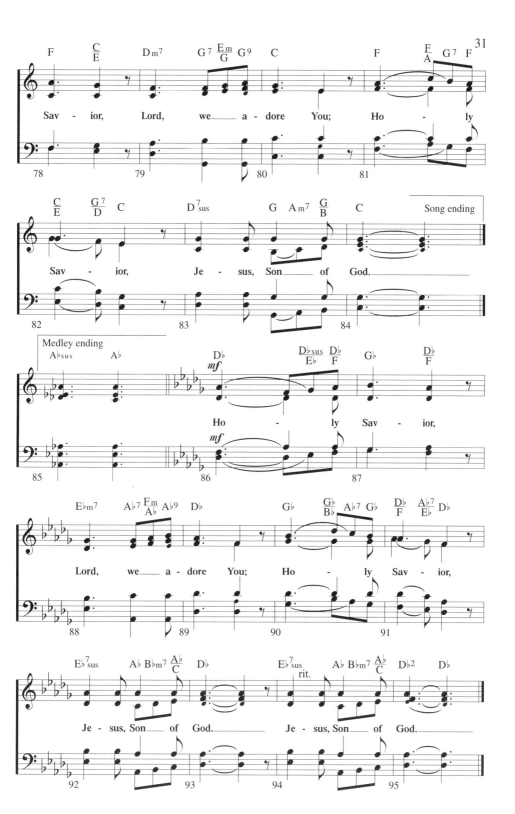

GO TELL IT!

includes
The Virgin Mary Had a Baby Boy
Go, Tell It on the Mountain

Presentation Suggestions:
THE VIRGIN MARY HAD A BABY BOY: Verse 1, unison; Refrain, parts; Verse 2,
ladies unison; Ms. 8, beat 4, men unison; Refrain, parts; Verse 3, choir unison;
Refrain, parts; Choral tag, parts
GO, TELL IT ON THE MOUNTAIN: Choir unison; Ms. 67, beat 3, parts

The Virgin Mary Had a Baby Boy

Traditional and
TOM FETTKE

Traditional
Arranged by Tom Fettke
and Camp Kirkland

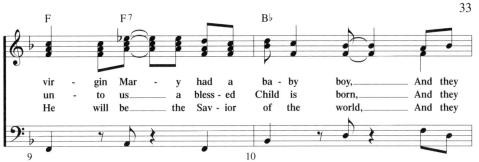

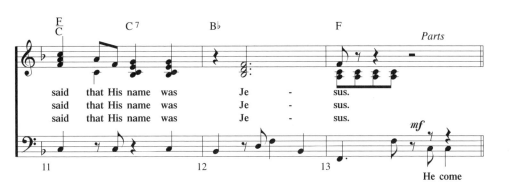

Go, Tell It on the Mountain

JOHN W WORK, JR.

Afro-American Spiritual
Arranged by Tom Fettke

KING OF KINGS ADORED

includes
Sovereign Lord
I Extol You
Holy Is the Lord

Presentation Suggestions:
SOVEREIGN LORD: 1st time, unison, 1st ending; 2nd time, parts, medley ending
I EXTOL YOU: 1st time, unison, song ending; 2nd time, ladies unison; Ms. 25, beat 4,
    choir unison, medley ending
HOLY IS THE LORD: Parts

Sovereign Lord

Words and Music by
TOM FETTKE

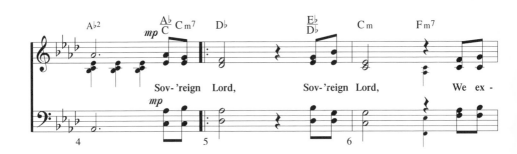

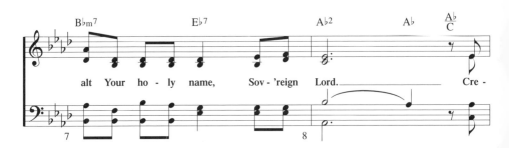

I Extol You

Words and Music by
JENNIFER RANDOLPH

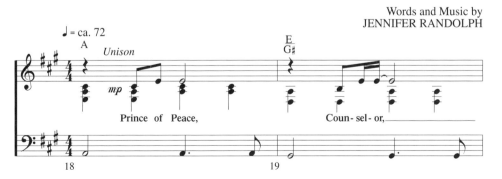

40

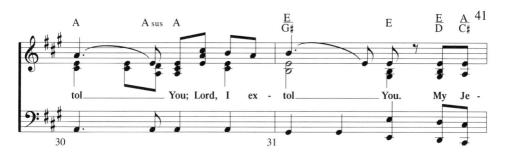

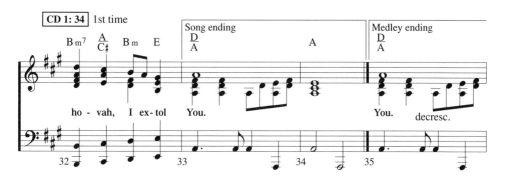

Holy Is the Lord

KEN BIBLE and
Traditional

FRANZ SCHUBERT
Arranged by Tom Fettke

THE STAR

includes
Behold the Star
The Star Carol

Presentation Suggestions:
BEHOLD THE STAR: Refrain, 2 times, parts; Verse 1, solo and choir parts (as
designated in song); Refrain, parts, song ending; Verse 2, solo and choir parts, medley
ending; Verse 3, solo and choir parts; Refrain, 2 times, parts, medley ending
THE STAR CAROL: Verse 1, parts, song ending; Verse 2, Soprano sing words, parts Oo,
medley ending; Verse 3, parts

Behold the Star

KEN BIBLE and
Traditional

Traditional Spiritual
Arranged by Tom Fettke

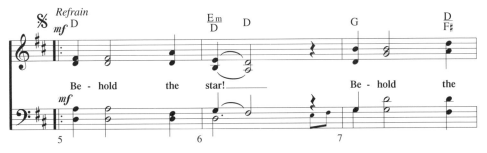

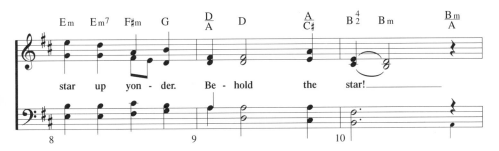

44

The Star Carol

WIHLA HUTSON

ALFRED BURT

48

CD 1: 41 1st time

CD 1: 42 2nd time

sleep____ on a bed of hay.
light____ 'round His lit - tle bed.
al - ways I'll think of Thee.

70   71   72   73

3. Dear Ba - by Je - sus, how____ ti - ny Thou art,____

74   75   76   77

I'll make a place for____ Thee____ in my heart,

78   79   80   81

And when the stars in the heav - ens I see,

82   83   84   85

Ev - er and al - ways I'll think of Thee.

86   87   88   89

GLORY, LOVE, AND PRAISE

includes
Joyful, Joyful, We Adore You
Light Is Shining All Around
O Hearken Ye

Presentation Suggestions:
JOYFUL, JOYFUL, WE ADORE YOU: Verse 1, parts, song ending; Verse 2, unison, medley ending
LIGHT IS SHINING ALL AROUND: Verse 1, ladies unison; Refrain, choir parts, song ending; Verse 2, men unison; Refrain, choir parts, medley ending
O HEARKEN YE: Verse 1, unison, song ending; Verse 3, parts, choral tag

Joyful, Joyful, We Adore You

LINDA LEE JOHNSON

LUDWIG VAN BEETHOVEN
Adapted by Edward Hughes

50

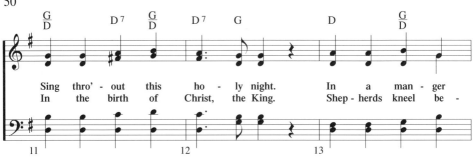

Sing thro' - out this ho - ly night. In a man - ger
In the birth of Christ, the King. Shep - herds kneel be -

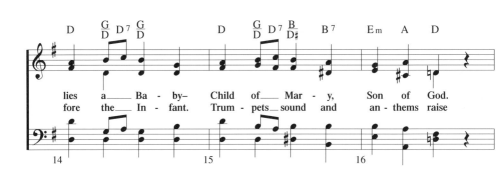

lies a___ Ba - by– Child of___ Mar - y, Son of God.
fore the___ In - fant. Trum - pets___ sound and an - thems raise

CD 1: 44 1st time   CD 1: 45 2nd time

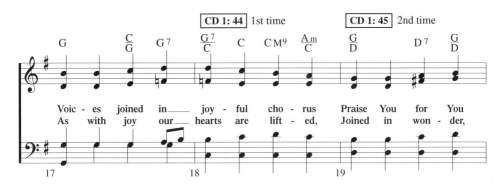

Voic - es joined in___ joy - ful cho - rus Praise You for You
As with joy our___ hearts are lift - ed, Joined in won - der,

Song ending   Medley ending

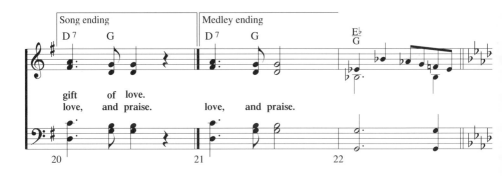

gift of love.
love, and praise.   love, and praise.

Light Is Shining All Around

Tune: *Ding, Dong, Merrily on High*

KEN BIBLE

Traditional and
KEN BIBLE

1. Light is shin-ing all a-round– The blaze of God's own glo-ry! Hear the an-gels fill the sky With joy in song and sto-ry: Glo - ri-a! Glo - ri-a!
2. "Peace and joy to all the earth, For God has shown His fa-vor: Born to you this ho-ly night A Child, a Son, a Sav-ior!"
3. Come, and see the Ho-ly Child, This won-der God has giv-en. Wor-ship now the in-fant Lord, The life and joy of heav-en.

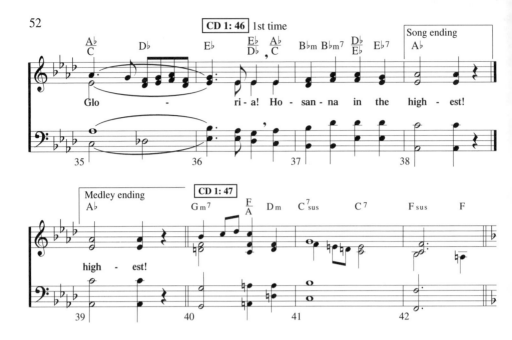

O Hearken Ye

WIHLA HUTSON

ALFRED BURT

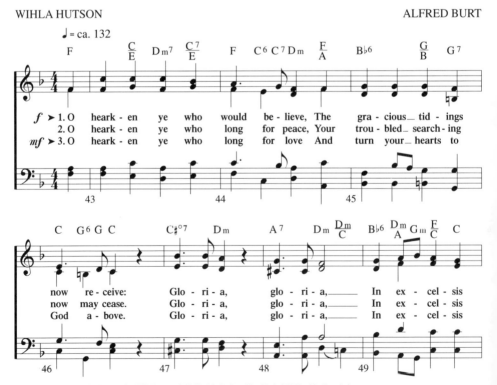

CHRISTMAS LAMB

includes
The Lamb of Christmas
Infant Holy, Infant Lowly

Presentation Suggestions:
    THE LAMB OF CHRISTMAS: Verse 1, parts, song ending; Verse 2, unison, song
    ending; Verse 5, parts, choral tag
    INFANT HOLY, INFANT LOWLY: Verse 1, unison; Ms. 41, beat 3, parts, song ending;
    Verse 2, parts, choral tag

The Lamb of Christmas

Tune: *The Friendly Beasts*

KEN BIBLE and
Traditional

French Melody, 13th c.
Arranged by Tom Fettke

1. "Come," said the lamb to the Ho - ly Child. "Come
2. "Come," said the song from the mid - night sky. "We'll
3. "Come," said the star so daz - zling bright. "We'll
4. Wise men brought gifts and gath - ered round. They
5. "Come," is the call of the Ho - ly Child. "Come

share my straw and rest a - while. Come,
sing through - out the world to - night, 'All
shine out peace and love and light! We'll
bowed their heads with - out a sound And
share My straw and rest a - while. You'll

Infant Holy, Infant Lowly

Polish Carol;
para. by Edith M. G. Reed

Polish Carol
Arranged by Tom Fettke

1. In-fant ho - ly, In-fant low - ly, For His bed— a cat - tle stall; Ox - en low - ing, lit - tle know - ing Christ, the Babe, is Lord of all. Swift are wing - ing an - gels

2. Flocks were sleep - ing; shep-herds keep - ing Vig - il till the morn-ing new Saw the glo - ry, heard the sto - ry— Tid - ings of a gos - pel true. Thus re - joic - ing, free from

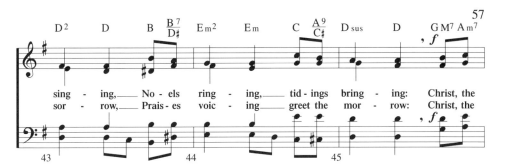

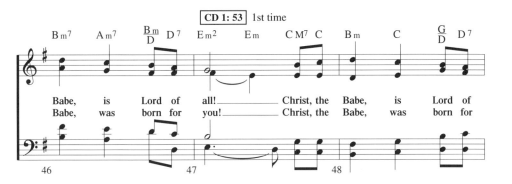

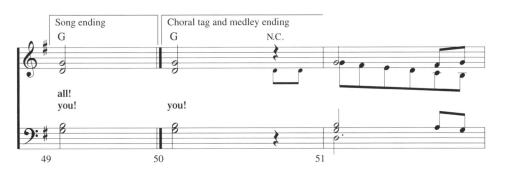

CELEBRATE THE COMING KING

includes

Lift Up Your Heads
Come, Thou Long-expected Jesus
Celebrate the Child

Presentation Suggestions:
LIFT UP YOUR HEADS: 1st time, unison, 1st ending; 2nd time, parts, medley ending
COME, THOU LONG-EXPECTED JESUS: Verse 1, ladies unison; Ms. 44, men unison,
song ending; Verse 3, parts, medley ending
CELEBRATE THE CHILD: Unison; Ms. 85, beat 4, parts

Lift Up Your Heads

Words and Music by
STEVE FRY

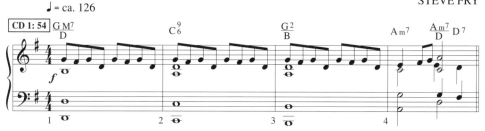

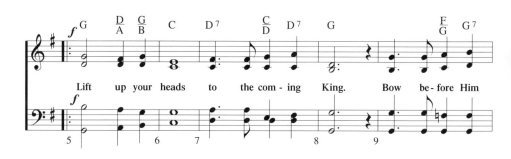

Medley Sequence copyright © 1998 by Pilot Point Music (ASCAP). All rights reserved.
Administered by The Copyright Company, 40 Music Square East, Nashville, TN 37203.

Come, Thou Long-expected Jesus

CHARLES WESLEY
and KEN BIBLE

ROWLAND H. PRICHARD

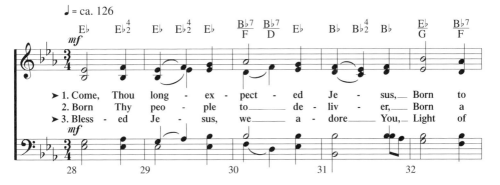

Celebrate the Child

Words and Music by
MICHAEL CARD

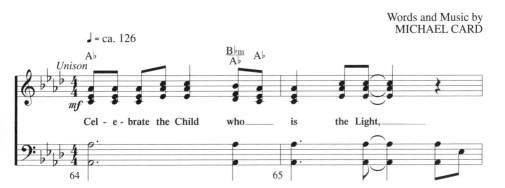

LET'S GO CAROLING

includes
Caroling, Caroling
Joy to the World
How Great Our Joy!

Presentation Suggestions:
CAROLING, CAROLING: Verse 1, unison
JOY TO THE WORLD: Verse 1, parts, song ending; Verse 2, unison, song ending;
Verse 3, parts, medley ending
CAROLING, CAROLING (Reprise I): Unison, medley ending
HOW GREAT OUR JOY!: Verse 1, men unison; Pick-up to ms. 82, choir parts, song
ending; Verse 2, ladies unison; Pick-up to ms. 82, choir parts, song ending; Verse 3,
choir parts, medley ending
CAROLING, CAROLING (Reprise II): Unison, choral tag

Caroling, Caroling

WIHLA HUTSON

ALFRED BURT

Joy to the World

ISAAC WATTS

GEORGE FREDERICK HANDEL
Arranged by Lowell Mason

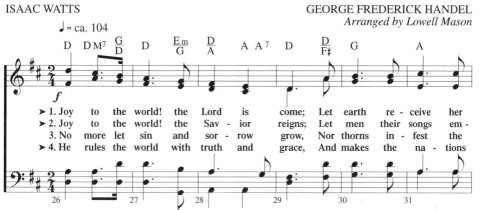

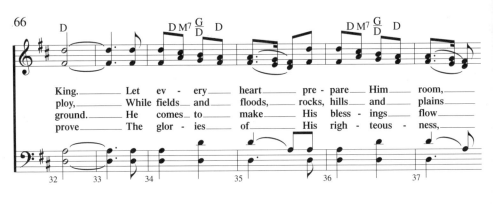

King.___ Let ev - ery___ heart___ pre - pare___ Him___ room,
ploy,___ While fields___ and___ floods,___ rocks, hills___ and___ plains
ground.___ He comes to___ make___ His bless - ings___ flow
prove___ The glor - ies___ of___ His righ - teous - ness,___

And heav'n and na - ture___ sing, And___ heav'n and na - ture___
Re - peat the sound - ing___ joy, Re - peat the sound - ing___
Far as the curse is___ found, Far___ as the curse is___
And won - ders of His___ love, And___ won - ders of His___

1. And heav'n and na - ture sing,___
1. And heav'n and na - ture sing, And

| CD 2: 3 | 1st time |
| CD 2: 4 | 2nd time |

Song ending

sing, And___ heav'n,___ and heav'n___ and na - ture___ sing.
joy, Re - peat,___ re - peat___ the sound - ing___ joy.
found, Far___ as,___ far as___ the curse is___ found.
love, And___ won - ders, won - ders of His___ love.

heav'n and na - ture sing,

CD 2: 5

♩ = ♩. Same tempo ♩. = ca. 104

Medley ending

love. mf

Caroling, Caroling
Reprise I

WIHLA HUTSON   ALFRED BURT

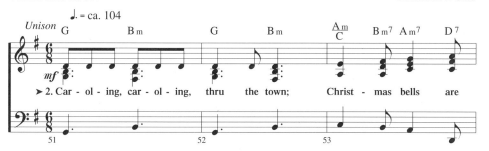

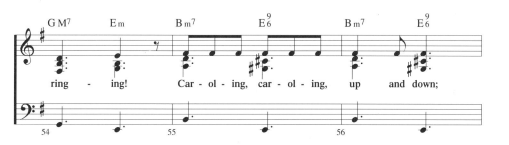

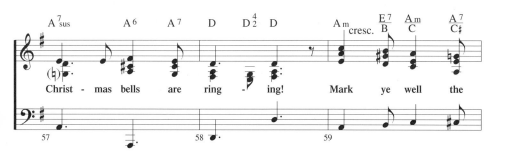

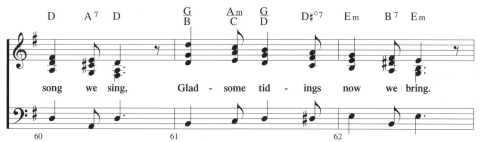

Ding, dong, ding, dong, Christ - mas bells are ring - ing. *mf*

Medley ending

ring - ing.

J = J Same tempo J = ca. 104

CD 2: 6

How Great Our Joy!

Traditional German Carol
Arranged by Hugo Jungst

J = ca. 104

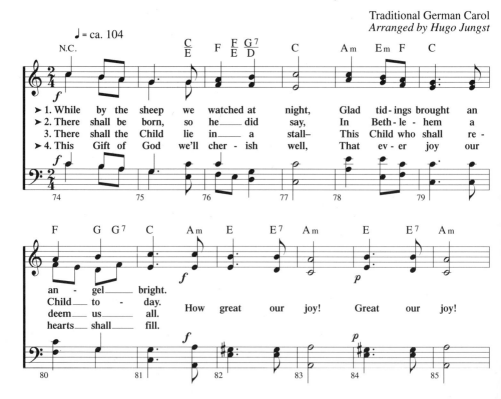

➤ 1. While by the sheep we watched at night, Glad tid - ings brought an
➤ 2. There shall be born, so he___ did say, In Beth - le - hem a
3. There shall the Child lie in___ a stall— This Child who shall re -
➤ 4. This Gift of God we'll cher - ish well, That ev - er joy our

an - gel___ bright.
Child___ to - day.   How great our joy! Great our joy!
deem___ us___ all.
hearts___ shall___ fill.

Caroling, Caroling
Reprise II

WIHLA HUTSON

ALFRED BURT

LET US ADORE HIM

includes
Gesu Bambino
Jesus

Presentation Suggestions:
GESU BAMBINO: Verse 1, solo (or unison); Pick-up to Ms. 7, parts; Ms. 13, unison
Verse 2, solo (or unison); Pick-up to Ms. 7, parts; Ms. 13, unison, medley ending
JESUS: Verse 1, parts; Verse 3, parts, 3rd ending

Gesu Bambino

FREDERICK H. MARTENS
and KEN BIBLE

PIETRO A. YON
Arranged by Tom Fettke

74

Jesus

Tune: *Jesu, Joy of Man's Desiring*

KEN BIBLE

JOHANN SCHOP
Adapted by J. S. Bach

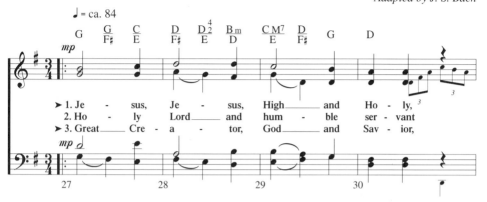

1. Je - sus, Je - sus, High and Ho - ly,
2. Ho - ly Lord and hum - ble ser - vant
3. Great Cre - a - tor, God and Sav - ior,

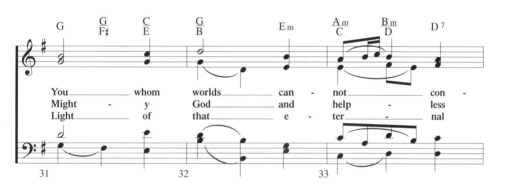

You whom worlds can - not con -
Might - y God and help - less
Light of that e - ter - nal

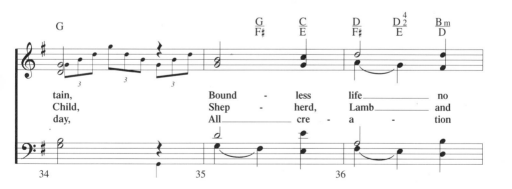

tain, Bound - less life no
Child, Shep - herd, Lamb and
day, All cre - a - tion

STAR OF WONDER

includes
We Three Kings
Beautiful Star of Bethlehem

Presentation Suggestions:
WE THREE KINGS: Refrain, parts, medley ending
BEAUTIFUL STAR OF BETHLEHEM: Verse 1 and Refrain, parts, 1st ending;
Verse 2, ladies unison; Ms.27, beat 4, men unsion; Refrain, parts, medley ending

We Three Kings

Words and Music by
JOHN H. HOPKINS, JR.
Arranged by Tom Fettke

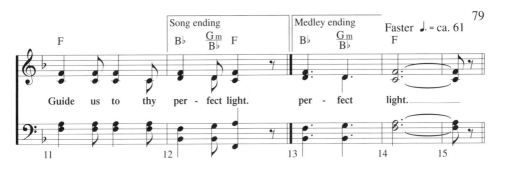

Beautiful Star of Bethlehem

ADGER M. PACE   CD 2: 15   1st time   R. FISCHER BOYCE

♩. = ca. 61   CD 2: 16   2nd time

1. O beau - ti - ful star of Beth - le - hem, shin - ing a -
2. O beau - ti - ful star, the hope of light, guid - ing the
3. O beau - ti - ful star, the hope of rest for the re -

far thro' sha - dows dim, Giv - ing a light for those who
pil - grim thro' the night, O - ver the moun - tain till the
deemed, the good and blessed, Yon - der in glo - ry when the

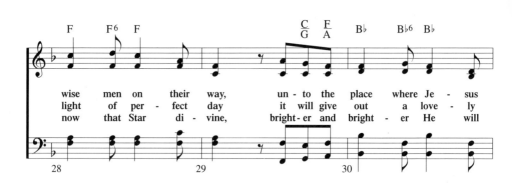

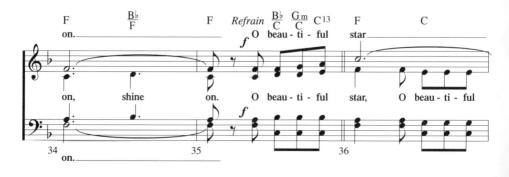

82

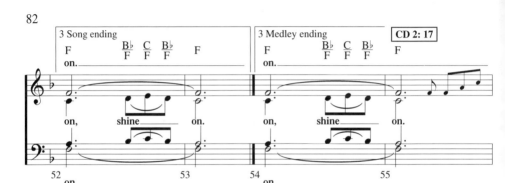

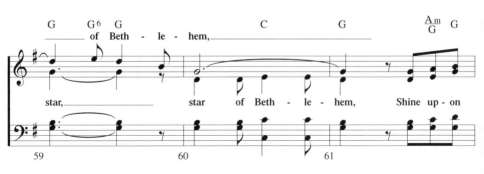

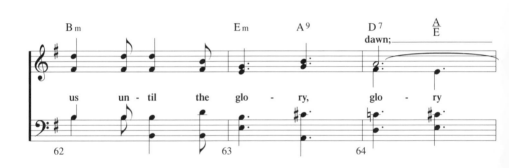

THE ANGEL CALLED HIM JESUS

includes

His Name Is Life
I Call Him Lord
That Beautiful Name

Presentation Suggestions:
HIS NAME IS LIFE: First time, unison, song ending; Second time, parts, medley ending
I CALL HIM LORD: Verse 1, solo; Refrain, choir parts, 1st ending; Verse 2, unison;
Refrain, parts, medley ending
THAT BEAUTIFUL NAME: Parts, medley ending

His Name Is Life

Words and Music by
CARMAN, GLORIA GAITHER,
and WILLIAM J. GAITHER

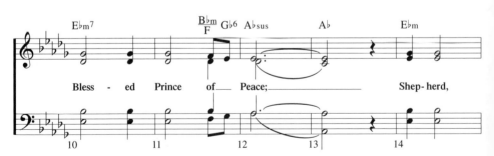

Medley Sequence copyright © 1998 by Pilot Point Music (ASCAP). All rights reserved.
Administered by The Copyright Company, 40 Music Square East, Nashville, TN 37203.

I Call Him Lord

Words and Music by
DOTTIE RAMBO

That Beautiful Name

JEAN PERRY, alt.

MABEL JOHNSTON CAMP
Arranged by Tom Fettke

DAY OF JOY
includes
It Came upon the Midnight Clear
Our Day of Joy
Good Christian Men, Rejoice

Presentation Suggestions:
IT CAME UPON THE MIDNIGHT CLEAR: Verse 1, unison, song ending; Verse 4, parts, medley ending
OUR DAY OF JOY: Verse 1, men unison; Refrain, choir parts, song ending; Verse 3, ladies unison; Refrain, choir parts, medley ending
GOOD CHRISTIAN MEN, REJOICE: Verse 1, unison, song ending; Verse 2, parts, choral tag

It Came upon the Midnight Clear

EDMUND H. SEARS

RICHARD C. WILLIS
Arranged by Tom Fettke

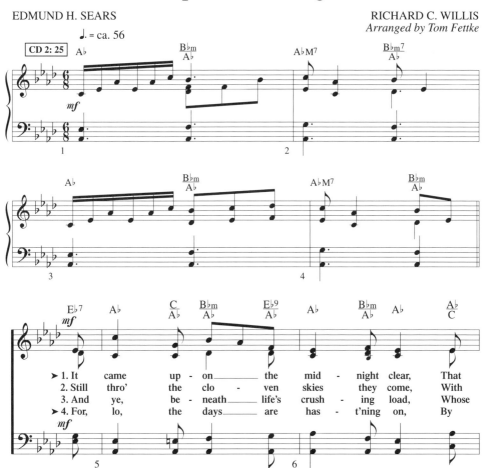

still - ness lay To hear the an - gels sing.
ba - bel sounds The bless - ed an - gels sing.
wea - ry road And hear the an - gels sing.
back the song Which now the an - gels sing.

Our Day of Joy

Words and Music by
ANDREW L. SKOOG
Arranged by Tom Fettke

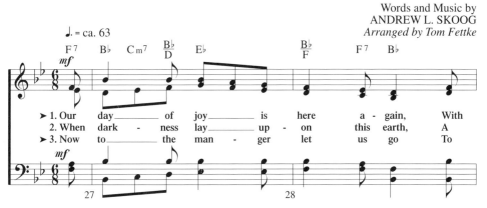

1. Our day of joy is here a - gain, With
2. When dark - ness lay up - on this earth, A
3. Now to the man - ger let us go To

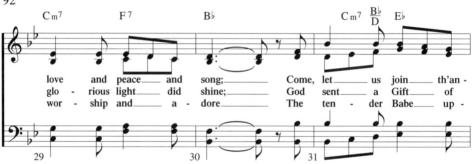

love and peace and song; Come, let us join th'an-
glo - rious light did shine; God sent a Gift of
wor - ship and a - dore The ten - der Babe up-

29   30   31

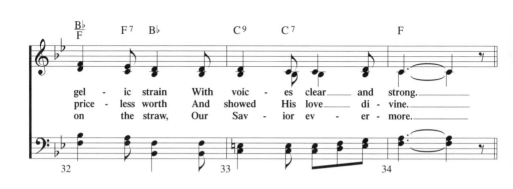

gel - ic strain With voic - es clear and strong.
price - less worth And showed His love di - vine.
on the straw, Our Sav - ior ev - er - more.

32   33   34

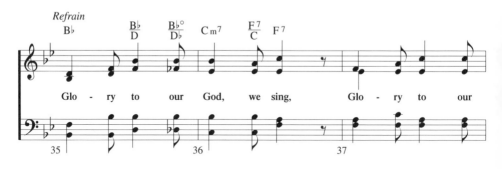

Refrain

Glo - ry to our God, we sing, Glo - ry to our

35   36   37

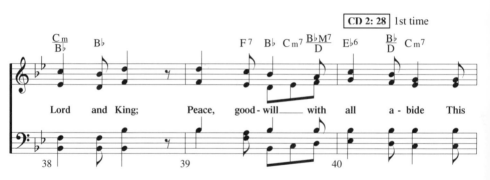

CD 2: 28 | 1st time

Lord and King; Peace, good - will with all a - bide This

38   39   40

Good Christian Men, Rejoice

Latin Carol, 14th c.
tr. by John M. Neale

Traditional German Carol, 14th c.
Arranged by Tom Fettke

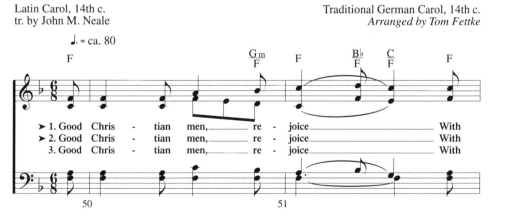

➤ 1. Good Chris - tian men,_____ re - joice_____ With
➤ 2. Good Chris - tian men,_____ re - joice_____ With
3. Good Chris - tian men,_____ re - joice_____ With

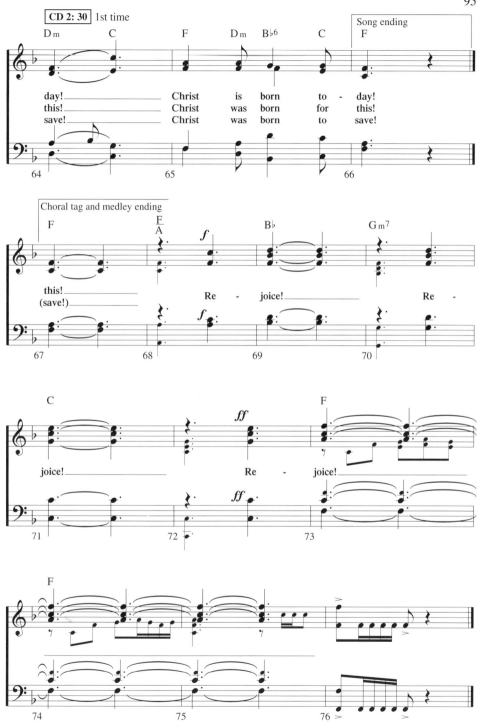

HOLY CHILD OF BETHLEHEM

includes
O Little Town of Bethlehem
The Birthday of a King
Gloria

Presentation Suggestions:
O LITTLE TOWN OF BETHLEHEM: Verse 1, parts, song ending; Verse 4, unison,
medley ending
THE BIRTHDAY OF A KING: Verse 1, ladies unison; Refrain, choir parts, song ending;
Verse 2, solo; Refrain, choir parts, medley ending
GLORIA: Parts, choral tag

O Little Town of Bethlehem

PHILLIPS BROOKS

LEWIS H. REDNER
Arranged by Tom Fettke

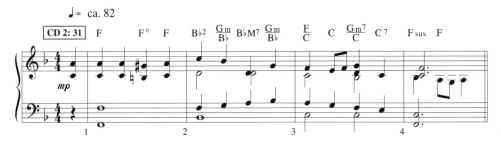

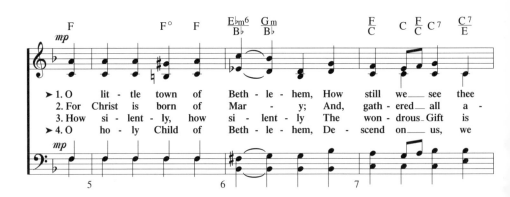

The Birthday of a King

Words and Music by
W. H. NEIDLINGER
Arranged by Tom Fettke

Gloria

Words and Music by
OTIS SKILLINGS

100

GOLD, FRANKINCENSE, AND MYRRH

includes
The March of the Three Wise Men
Adoration

Presentation Suggestions:
  THE MARCH OF THE THREE WISE MEN: Verse 1, men unison; Pick-up to ms. 13,
  choir unison, song ending; Verse 2, ladies unison; Pick-up to ms. 13, choir unison,
  medley ending
  ADORATION: Verse 1, parts, song ending; Verse 2, parts, choral tag

The March of the Three Wise Men

KEN BIBLE

French Melody
Arranged by Tom Fettke

1. Three wise men, in - spir - ed by a star, Pre -
2. Three wise men, led on - ly by a star, Ar -

102

Adoration

JOHN S. B. MONSELL
and KEN BIBLE

TOM FETTKE

YOUR LIGHT HAS COME

includes
Arise, Shine
He's Still the King of Kings

Presentation Suggestions:
ARISE, SHINE: Sing two times, unison, medley ending 2nd time
HE'S STILL THE KING OF KINGS: Verse 1, parts; Refrain, parts, song ending; Verse
2, unison; Refrain, parts, choral tag

Arise, Shine

Words and Music by
STEVE URSPRINGER
and JAY ROBINSON

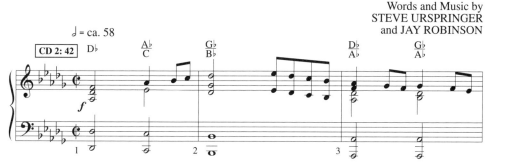

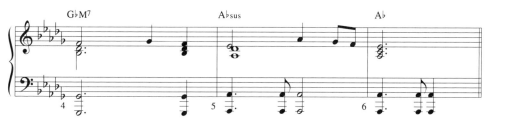

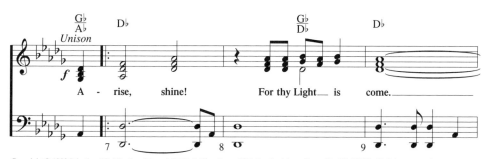

A - rise, shine! For thy Light is come.

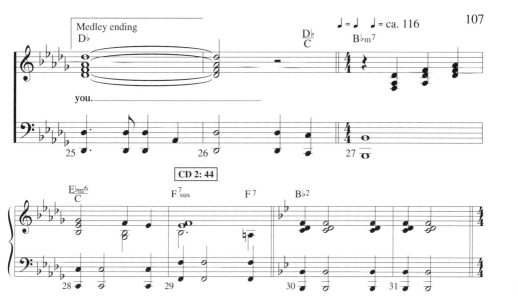

He's Still the King of Kings

GLORIA GAITHER,
WILLIAM J. GAITHER
and RONN HUFF

WILLIAM J. GAITHER

FOR UNTO US A CHILD IS BORN

includes
His Glorious Name
Wonderful Counselor

Presentation Suggestions:
HIS GLORIOUS NAME: Unison; Ms. 12, parts, medley ending
WONDERFUL COUNSELOR: 1st time, unison; Ms. 50, parts, song ending; 2nd time,
unison; Ms. 50, parts, choral tag; Ms. 66, unison; Ms. 75, parts

His Glorious Name

Adapted from Isaiah 9:6

JEAN SIBELIUS
Arranged by Tom Fettke

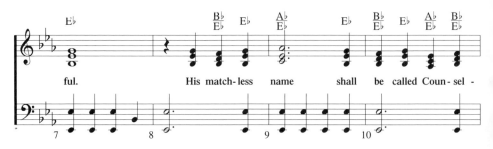

Wonderful Counselor

Words and Music by
JOHN MICHAEL TALBOT

For un-to us a Child is born, a Son is giv-en. Come Holy Spir-it, come fa-ther this Child. The Vir-gin Mar-y shall be His moth-er,

114

In the First Light

Words and Music by
BOB KAUFLIN
Arranged by Tom Fettke

1. In the first light of a new day no one knew He had ar - rived. Things con - tin - ued as they had been while a new - born soft - ly cried. But the

CD 2: 50

heav-ens wrapped in won-der knew the mean-ing of His

birth; In the weak-ness of a ba-by they knew

God had come to earth.

2. As His moth-er held Him close-ly it was

hard to un-der-stand That her ba-by, not yet

MERRY CHRISTMAS

includes
Here We Come Rejoicing
We Wish You a Merry Christmas

Presentation Suggestions:
HERE WE COME REJOICING: Verse 1, unison; Refrain, parts, song ending; Verse 2,
unison; Refrain, parts, medley ending
WE WISH YOU A MERRY CHRISTMAS: Unison; Ms. 46, beat 3, parts, medley
ending

Here We Come Rejoicing

KEN BIBLE and
Traditional

English Folk Song
Arranged by Tom Fettke

We Wish You a Merry Christmas

KEN BIBLE and
Traditional

Traditional English Melody
Arranged by Tom Fettke

TOPICAL INDEX

ALPHABETICAL INDEX

Song and *Medley* Titles